A MOTHER CARRIES

POEMS

by bec ellis

love,
bec ellis

bec ellis

Copyright © 2022 bec ellis

All rights reserved. No part of this book may be reproduced or used in any manner without the prior written permission of the copyright owner, except for the use of brief quotations in a book review.

To request permission, contact the copyright owner at contact@bec-ellis.com

ISBN: 978-0-578-37287-7

First paperback edition: March 25th, 2022

Self-published. Photographs & design by bec ellis.

DEDICATION

mother isn't just a title
or noun; it is the strongest
verb I know

// to all who mother

// womb

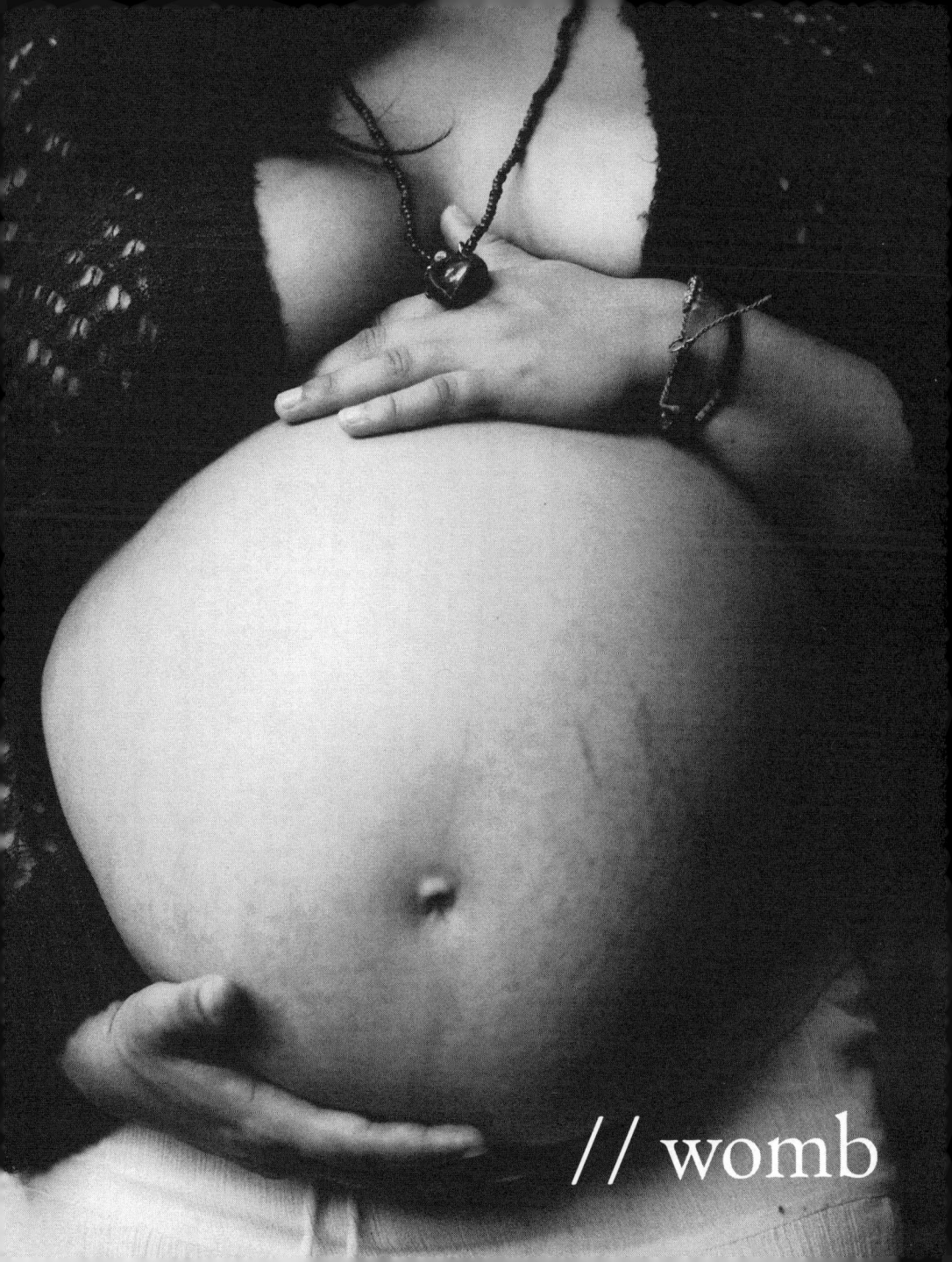

first, it was the unknown
the waiting
and then, those
twin lines
feared or hoped for
the scream
of excitement -
or maybe, terror -
the egg
sperm
exploding cells
embryo
sickness
fatigue
pale skin
pretending to just
be under
the weather.
then the fetus,
heartbeat,
thump-thump-thump,
four chambers
tests and decisions
and more waiting;
scans and appointments,
elastic waists
and the stretching
and swelling
of skin and body
becoming more obvious
each day.

and then, the telling -
to everyone
about what is coming,

and the congratulations
and good wishes
and sullen reminders
of how your life
will change
forever -
you hope you didn't speak
too soon.
smiles, tears, hugs
disapproving looks
and blank stares
and all the terror stories
and unhelpful advice
you could never
have asked for.
flutters, kicks
a hand resting
against your now solid belly,
waiting to feel the pulse,
to connect in some way
with this being growing
inside of you -
together you wait
and carry on.

the appointments
keep coming,
the kicks are stronger now -
you wonder if you can
really
expand
that
much
more, rearrange
any more organs

or bedroom furniture
create enough room
for this tiny human.
heartburn,
insomnia,
sciatic nerves,
did she kick today?
did you take your vitamins?
is your birth plan ready?
have you
checked
off
every
box
and also
made sure to take
care of yourself?
go and relax
a little
have some fun
while creating
a human being,
like it's no big task
at all.

the due date looms ahead -
or maybe it is
taking forever
to arrive
they keep saying
you are glowing
but also,
with raised eyebrows,
can you get any bigger?
or maybe

you are not big enough,
is she still growing in there?
are you already failing
at being a mother?

the day comes
and somehow
this tiny life is born,
by miracle and mercy
and some sort of
magic you think, too.
she is resting in your arms now,
snug in the blanket
that one friend bought,
and everything inside
wants to settle -
but you are leaky
and soft still
and need to be
wrapped tightly,
too.
everyone wants to know
if the baby is healthy
weight
length
head size
apgar
cell phone photo
another list
to complete,
but don't they realize
that you
have just been born
as well?
and now you hold

this wrinkled, fleshy
version of yourself
and realize
how
much
you have been carrying,
how
much
more
you have to hold,
like
this messy heart
broken open
and
expanding
in ways
you never knew
and will never
fully
understand.

// a mother carries

my body
this vessel
your heart
my soul -
where does one end
and the other begin?

you grew here
in this womb
brilliant and silent,
you somehow
stitched me back together
in ways
I didn't even know
I needed.

// this startling symbiosis

do you feel it?
each fiber
ligament, cell -
stretched and pulled
up, down
over, through;
woven together
into this masterpiece.

// a stunning tapestry (aka you)

am I carrying you
or are you
carrying me?
I wonder
as I lean into
this sacred dance
of surrender and strength,
watch our bodies form
one another
breath-by-breath and
cell-by-cell,
both of us
in the process of
becoming,
both of us learning
how to live into
this strange new
existence.

// intertwined

// undoing

now you are here
in my arms
and
I'm falling apart
again.

// after-birth

is this love or grief
or pain or joy
or just the reality of
uncertainty
in motherhood?
this is the part
no one prepares you for

that this thing
you so desperately ached for
you now must ache through

this life you carried
for so long, now
bundled in your arms
against your sore breasts
and loose body,
a labor and birth
of its own -
you are complete
and incomplete
all at once,
unraveling
and just being made.

// the unmaking of motherhood

our skin
slides together,
melts into our
curves, meets
for the first time
like we've always
known one another.

// skin to skin

how come
no one ever told me
that when I held you
I would begin the process
of becoming completely
undone
that as I attempt to weave
you into the threads
of my own life
an entire new pattern
would emerge -
impossibly intricate
stunningly beautiful
even while imperfect -
and I'm left wondering,
looking for even a trace
of what was before.

no one explained to me
that my heart would break
like the life water
that enfolded you
nothing can hold back
these rushing waves
expanding within me
breaking me open
showing me
how love is found
in these cracks
desperate and moving
in a way I don't understand.

so I sit here
unraveling and still whole
asking as our skin meets:

how do you do it?
break me apart
while at the same time
be the only thing
keeping me together?

// breaking apart or breaking open?

I've learned that you
can love being a mother
while also questioning
what you gave up
to become one, that
you can revel in
the softness of your
child's flesh against
your body
while also wanting
your skin to just be
your own again, that
you can feel like
some hidden part inside of you
has been made more whole
while also never feeling
like you are quite
enough.

// w(hole)

do you feel it
this break, these cracks
this impossible expansion -

my very being
breaking open
to make space
for you.

// beauty in the breaking

the mirror seems to define you as so soft and tender, even
your under garments point out how loose your body has
become, how it begs to be bound back together.
but these words don't describe you at all, do they? my dear
warrior-mother, who pushed life through water and fire.
who bears the marks and scars of one who has roared through labor, whether
with quiet rhythmic sighs or fierce battle cries - you are anything but soft

and it seems everyone loves to celebrate the war hero –
or at least her shiny medal, swaddled on her chest
all she has to show for her great sacrifice -
but then, the headlines fade and the world just turns
again as normal

society loves to forget the wounds
that still need to heal
the ones that never will
all while expecting life
to go on as before.

// but is the baby healthy?

of course we are soft
because motherhood
requires it, this thing
that is equal parts unexplainable gift
and cruel trick
that will break us until
we learn when and how
to shift and bend, this thing
that carries us as we
carry it.

// flow

they told me
motherhood would
change me like
nothing I've ever known,
that I would finally
understand once I
had given birth.
I thought I was
prepared, had read
the books and knew exactly
how my children would
never act in public
but here I am
holding this babe, this life
made up of
salt
water
love
all wrapped up
a little too seriously
in flesh-from-my-own-flesh and
it all feels beautifully unclear -
this stunning invitation into
something impossible to name.
but perhaps there are words
only our bodies understand,
maybe that's what they were trying
to tell me all along -
how once you have given birth
to something you weren't
strong enough to hold
before,
everything changes.

// the unsettling clarity of motherhood

slow and all at once
you are now the one
being knit back
together,
stitch
by
stitch
by
stitch.

// postpartum

who knew embracing
this skin would be
such an act of
rebellion?

// stretched

in those early
waking
heavy-eyelid hours
when the house
is quietly humming
like your body
soft and steady
I find myself awake
and alert
just watching
the stunning reality
of your existence.

// the real reason I am always tired

now you must
watch
this tiny being existing
so small and brave
and pink
in the world,
as their stitches become
snagged or stretched
or pulled out completely,
unfolding a new pattern
never imagined,
grief and love and
marvel mingling
in your heart,
your eyes.
you must decide
what to do
with your own
heart and hands
as you look on,
let them live
into their own
wonderfully
complicated
existence, trust
the process
know you can't keep
them safe forever
but
you can always be
their safe place
whenever they
need to return.

// knit together

some days,
you may feel all
dried up and tired,
your body and heart
aching, rest a far
way off; your worn
raw skin crusting over
a heavy and dull weight
you can't set down.
you might look around
or in the mirror
feel unqualified
and less-than, hear the
whispers of disappointment
in your ears -
but how I wish
you could see yourself,
the brave way
you have surrendered,
how you show up
again and again with this love
pouring out
even when you feel
the most unlovely.

maybe then,
you might
be more gentle
with yourself.

// over-qualified

why didn't anyone tell me
that you could be so lonely
even when you're
never alone

that you can wonder
if you have any value
while constantly
being needed

that you can wear tiredness
heavy on your body
and not realize the weight of it
(until you finally get
that magical extra hour
of sleep)

that the name "mama" will
both stretch you to impossible
lengths and somehow
bring you home
to yourself

that a mother never really
sets down this
mantle and crown
even when she is desperate to,
even when she thinks
she doesn't deserve it –
instead, she rises.
again and again
and finds both her heartache
and relief in these long but
much too short days
and nights which ask

everything of her.

// the quiet and unnoticed strength of a mother

scared.
scarred.
sacrum.
sacred.

// a progression of becoming
(or maybe just understanding)

why does this mother-heart
have to be so complicated -
this fierce loving thing
that can be both intimately connected
and terrifyingly fearful, acting out
in ways I don't understand or
even knew were possible?

why do we have to hold so many
both-ands, so many opposing
hard-yet-easy things -
how can we be so strong
and impossibly tired at once?

but here is the grace I
have learned to walk in:

we can never be everything
to anyone
but we can always give
everything we have
in each
moment.

// the complicated joy of motherhood

oh the beauty of one
compelled to spill
themselves out
for another.

// mother

oh mother. I see you.
holding so much and barely dragging yourself along.
the ongoing list.
the fears and anxieties.
the making the best of it.
the constant ups and downs between feeling strong and capable,
and the unthinkable tiredness you wear.

how do we move forward
and how do we remember to bring ourselves along?
what do we do on the days we wonder how
to get back to ourselves, to reconnect with our babes and look and see
with eyes set on finding loveliness in both ourselves and others?
how do we remember
to not let ourselves simply be an after-thought
and what are we to do when we realize

there is no one there to hold us.

// there are many more questions than answers here.

perhaps the hardest work
a mother does, is learning
to love herself
just as she is.
even on this rough-flavored
morning when everything feels
hard
heavy
uncertain;
when she looks at her hands
and notices how tired they feel,
that maybe she has been holding
too much, after all.

it all feels impossible to set down;
so much of what she holds is
good. but at least, dear mother,
let go of this one small-appearing
heavy thing that you were never
meant to carry:

the belief that there is
something more you must
do
be
become
change
in order to love
and be loved.

// mothering ourselves

motherhood
is
breaking
while
mending

// a beautiful becoming

// ache

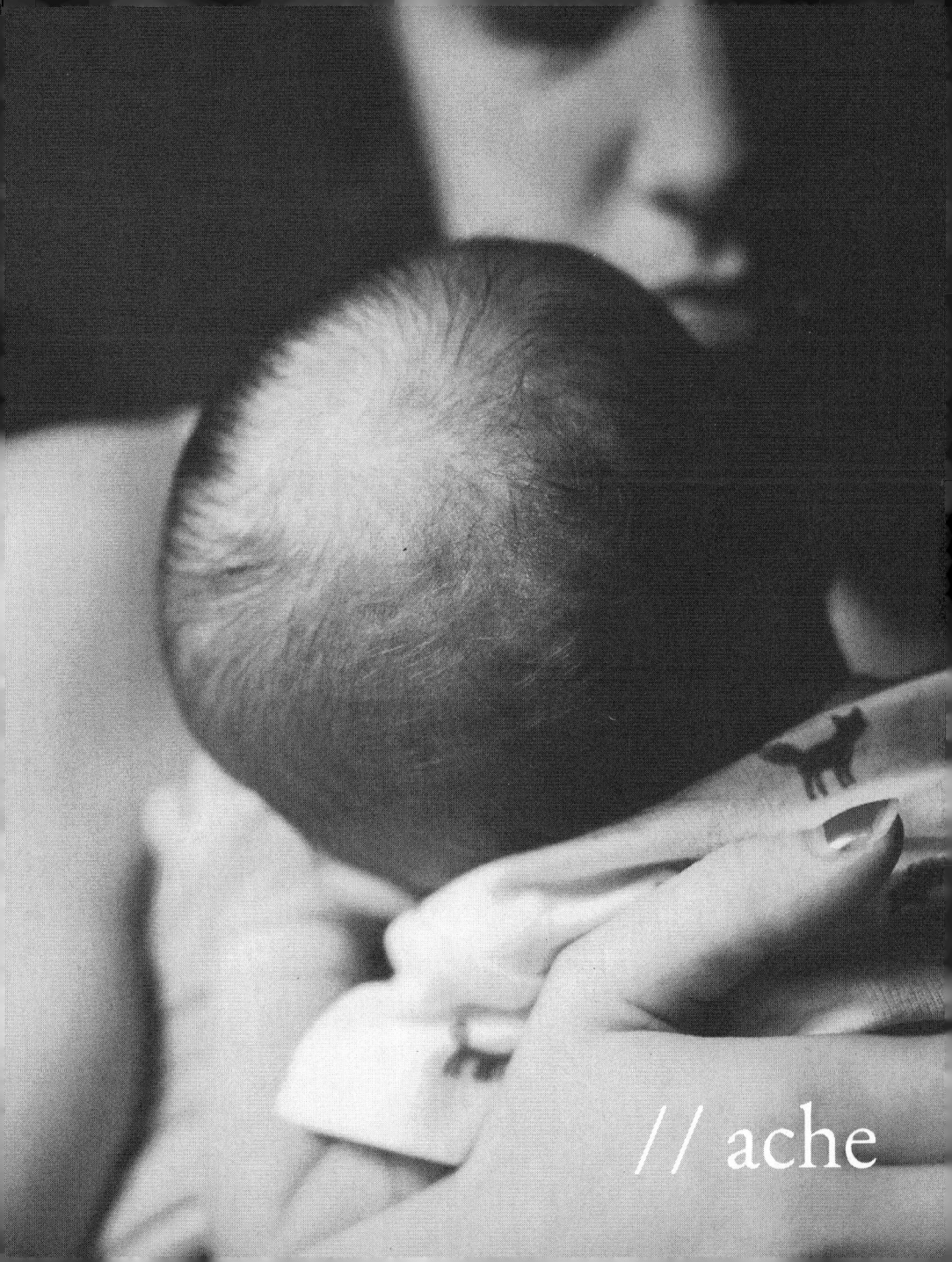

there is a mystery
I have discovered -
that you can hold
great sadness
and joy
and hope
all at once -
there are no rules
about it.

// a mother's ache

did the morning light
wake me
or is that you
as you slowly push the door
creaking it open
and walk, all smiles
and bed-tossed hair
across the room,
climb into bed
and hold my face
between your warm
and perfectly soft palms,
our lips curve up
as our noses meet,
I can't help but
stroke that little curl
on your forehead
and wonder
are you the last
of my babes
to crawl into our bed
still young and tender,
and at first light
remind me that I
am your everything?
wouldn't it be nice
if everyone could
start their day like that.

it makes me ache
to think of this
to be so aware
of the inevitable
"last time" -
there have been

so many of them
that have passed me by
will it be different now?
will I somehow know
tell myself
this is it?
will I slow and with
eyes looking wide, allow
this one dangling piece
of motherhood
to finally drift away?
will I remember
how right here
in this moment
I am so perfectly content
with you.

// the complicated grief of an empty womb

motherhood is
wondering when
things will get better
only to miss
when things seemed
so damn hard.

// the slow & quick phases

sometimes
the healing
is in the aching
and the loving
is most obvious
in the losing.

// I miss your heartbeat in my womb

things were supposed to be
so different, weren't they -
you, small and pink, breathing
on my chest
tiny fingers curled
around my own
instead, I'm wandering
these halls, eyes and breasts leaking
my body, longing to heal
both itself and you

my face is soaked in anger
and stolen moments
we will never know or
share, but even here -

I am reminded
how healing takes time,
that goodness
beauty
brokenness
are discovered around every corner
living together and all at once
in the same spaces,
breaking bread and growing
out of the cracks
of the other,
that anger
sadness
joy
gratitude
can exist on the same plane
that maybe this is what living
feels like, after all -
complicated

unthinkable
and irreverently hard -

but I'd rather feel it all
than become numb
to the memory
of you.

// feeling much too alive

it will be over soon,
the empyting.
daily I have
no appetite
like I must make
myself empty
feel the hunger pains
echo in this chamber
of grief
because my womb
is no longer
full.

// this sudden hollowness

maybe
it is because
I know you were the last one
that I feel so empty
now, never to feel
the magic of life
growing inside again -
and every month
I am reminded
with this ritual moon emptying
that my womb
is mourning
still.

// a mother's grief is not that simple

ever have those days
where you feel
like you are ripping
apart
at the seams?
where you just
aren't sure
you will ever
figure out
how to actually
be again?
there's this heavy
weepy sort of feeling
behind your eyes
but they stay dry
somehow,
tears held like a dam
has been placed there -
of course you have built one -
and all you want
is to hold your
sweet babe
softly remind them
that they are
brilliant
beyond words -
yet, there is this
painful distance
because you can't
even keep yourself
from falling apart.

// when will I be the mother I want to be

no one told me
how much love hurts,
that when I see
the joy in your eyes
it feels
like someone has
hold of my heart, wringing
every
last
drop
of love
out.
I feel it, like hot wax
sliding off a candle
and know
I will never
be the same again,
and each year
I become
a little more
weepy and wise
as it becomes
more clear
you won't be little
forever.
so I loosen my hold
and try to remember
the wonderful pain
of loving you
my child.

// a pain I cannot bear to live without

he is 9 months old now
breathing outside of me
as long as within
and the days go
quick
and slow
all at once.

like these milk-filled
breasts, there are moments
of feeling so full
nearly bursting
with joy and intense love
the fullness almost
makes me ache -
and then other times
I am so tired
the well feels drained,
the hollowness
overwhelming,
I feel nothing
and wonder
if I really know
how to love
at all.

// could it just be mood swings?

tonight
I breathe in
and know
the tiredness
my body holds.

// a mother's tired

what happens when
the mother breaks, when she
is there, right beside you
but a world away,
who is coming to save her -
is it you, small one?
how could such a
great task
meet you so very
early in life?

// I am sorry I am not more for you

I want to be held and left alone.
I want to sink into a dark room
and let the sun shine brightly
on my face.
I want to be the one who gently
cares for their needs and
not have to think about it for once.
I am light and heavy.
I am here and there.
I am strong and falling apart.
I am scared and brave.
I am isolated and never alone.
I am exhausted and ready.
I am caught in the in-between
something like birth, an eviction
of home, although
I can't leave these walls.
I am clinging to some hint of normalcy
the warm enclosure I am used
to being held in
and I wonder

what happens when we must emerge
into a new existence?
how do we stay alive while
moving toward this unknown?

// motherhood: a new normal

it's funny how you can
wake up dizzy
with life -
warm hands and
skin circle around you
hungry and soft all
at once -
and yet, your chest
quiet and hollow
makes you wonder
what being alive
really means
at all.

// loneliness

sometimes motherhood feels dried out and stale, like last seasons
dead blooms or the cereal that was left with the box flaps open and
exposed for weeks. we wonder what is next
and what we are even doing and how it is that we are trusted with
these beautiful and fierce children, these souls that we will leave a
mark on like no one else.

but how can we hold it all?

where do we find room left to store all the pieces of motherhood
when we feel both hollow and heavy?

somehow this heart continues breaking and expanding
again and again
and I must remind myself to not turn brittle with resentment
at all motherhood asks of me.

to remain soft and strong all at once.
and that it is okay
to feel so tired and worn in this moment.

I am not broken.
I am still here.
I am finding my way home again.

// still here

do they notice
when I am so tired
I can barely move -
my presence both
thick and distant
my eyes and heart
heavy
my words short
and flat. do they think it is
because of them - that I don't
quite love them enough, or
that they are somehow
inadequate, unable to make me
happy and light again?
this should never be
a child's chore,
to save their mother.

so I fight with all I have for them,
against the cruel voices
heavy limbs
weak eyes
wondering to myself
all the while
why am I always so tired?

// distance (or perhaps adrenal fatigue)

I know the fog will pass
eventually,
there is a strange and unknown
rhythm to it all -
but for now
I slowly roll out of bed and
stare out windows
and wonder
if this will ever not be
normal.

// a mother carries [on]

don't you see
all you are holding?
don't you see
that as mother
you are carrying
so much more than
just yourself
through this world?
that you are brave and strong
even while unraveling?
that motherhood is full
of complicated contradictions
and no one really knows
what is coming
when they place
the mantle of mother
upon their shoulders?

// unexpected weight

oh dear woman
how I wish
you could set down this
hard and heroic
way you have learned
to hold yourself in
all these years
and instead,

exhale.

// woman: a beautiful & resilient being

// desire

I sit here
at the dining room table
dinner crumbs
still scattered
on the surface,
evening light
dims the house.
I sit in the dark
except for the light
from the kitchen
where mountains
of dirty porcelain waits
to be washed.

they are in bed -
the children, and
so are you -
but here I am
all at once
feeling guilty
tired
lazy
free,
a mother with space
to sit and do
one
thing
her soul desires
but she isn't sure
what that is -

maybe it is the dishes
after all.

// a mother's freedom

motherhood is
loving your children fiercely
while asking
what
you
gave
up
to get here.

// but would you change anything?

some days
I feel like my
only hobbies are
snacking
cleaning the house
changing diapers
and feeling guilty.

// a question of purpose

when I try
to find my purpose
I have told my heart
it was too big to do
something so small
so domesticated
so simple -

*but nothing
is too small
for a big heart*

it whispered back.

// heart knows best

music
laughter
quiet
stillness
sunshine
skin on skin
softness
song
water
gentle
swaying
warmth
light
tenderness
understanding
time
less
more.

// a mother's wish list - 1 of 2

some days
my dreams amount
to nothing -
just wisps
in the air
a list, a chore
a task
check the box and
move onto
the next thing -
the sun still shines
somewhere
and the world turns

I am tired
and the eyes
do not lie,
I could sleep for
days uninterrupted
I settle
for mere hours
because a mother's life
is ever revolving,
so much sameness -
the rub is felt
over and over,
raw and defining.
I will emerge
one day
out of this fog
of young ones
deeply knowing
I am better for it ,
but for now
I write words

with eyes slowly battling
to stay alert,
begging to be closed,
a heavy load
bearing down
on my lashes
sleep is calling,
so I close my book
thoughts
dreams
loose ends
waiting to be finished.
I drift off
know in my bones
sleep will be short -
for a mother is always on call
even in the dark hours -
but for now
in this moment
I will rest
and trust the world
to keep spinning
and know
the words
sentences
dreams
will still be there
when I awake.

// a mother's dream

do you feel
loved
desired, even?
during these days
thick in the caring
of young ones
or after
when you look
in the mirror
and hardly
know yourself?

I know
I am loved
and desired
it is written
all over him,
the way his body moves
quickens inside,
his warm skin
drawn like a magnet to
my own, he can't help
but come close -
but I am nothing
just hollow eyes and
rough skin
he calls it soft
but I have
no
more
touch
to give.
I pull away,
instinctively now
but I wish I hadn't,

I wish I could let myself
stay and sink and settle
into this man
this home and harbor,
the one I have
set up house with
who I share
adventures
and children
and meals
and bonfires
and late nights
and too many glasses of
red wine with
still, I distance myself
listen to some
old lie,
one that has followed me
from childhood -
I wonder
am I really
desired?
he tries to leave
his shift early
just to gain
mere minutes more
by my side,
all the while
I lay here
and wonder
if another man
would still have me.

// to be desired

do you remember
those
young lovers
running unbridled
mostly fearless
and unswayed
toward the rest
of their lives
together?

here we are now
years in-between and
after growing-up some
wondering what
those kids were
thinking.

// I'm glad we didn't overthink it

is this where we
have come to exist -
we know each other
so well,
words are simply
accessories.

// date night after 15 years

once in a while,
I feel your hand
caress this old-mother skin
in a more noticing way

I wonder how something
can feel so soft
and tough and worn
all at the same moment,
how you can still see me -
want me, even -
with those lover's eyes,
gazing strong and innocent,
like it has been no time at all
since we fell hard for each other.

my eyes flutter shut
while my heart, alarmed
is begging me to melt
and settle, to allow
myself to be scooped up
and loved
like a babe who knows
no other reality.
oh, but it is hard
and feels impossible
at least, today
to really understand
my loveliness
like it needs to be unearthed,
gently, like a great artifact
excavated from somewhere
deep within my being.
so, you keep on looking
with those eyes of yours,

softly reminding me
that my beauty has only
deepened these years, that
my body has only
become more radiant,
glowing with story
and song,
carrying all the scents
and scars of the life
we have written together,
and you will be here
delicately brushing the dust off
until one day
I can finally see what you see.

// why have I buried my worth so deep?

how can he make
just one remark
maybe carelessly
not meaning a thing
and a fire rises in my chest
as I list
all
that
I
have
given
today
and wonder how this
same tired argument
has surfaced
yet again.

// the work of marriage

maybe tomorrow
things will look
less ugly
when the sun
is shining
and our hearts
are rested
and ready to
forgive again.

// new light

I hear your
rhythmic breathing
as I lay here
with my bedside light on
writing words
I don't know why
and I am struck with how
deeply grateful I am
that you are here with me
I feel your love radiate
even now, unspoken
almost unnoticed
and I know
you believe in me
like no one else.

// what would I do without you

how is it
that you like me
so much still
after all these years
together -
it feels like
almost more
than should be allowed
just one person

and all the while
I sit here
feeling plain
dull
worn
but you pull me in
lock my body against
your chest
as if we were made
for one another,
and you remind me again
of what my beauty
does to you.

// please keep reminding me

he showers me
with sonnets, still -
space for long runs on
lonely rugged trails,
time to let my creativity
run wild within,
freshly brewed tea
unexpected and hot
in my hands,
the smallest and most
tender of kisses
planted on my brow -
living love poems
you can't read
on a page or
write down in a book,
expressed through
heart-felt movement -

and yet
I still have
some quiet longing
for my heart to be
wooed again

I wait for my fairytale
only to miss the one
I am already living in.

// learning to choose him again like he chooses me

you find me
sleeves rolled up and
arms deep
in white foam,
back turned
as I face the spotted
kitchen window
that never seems
to get cleaned.
I wipe the hair
from my forehead,
a wetness left
on my cheek
and suddenly, you
wrap your arms
around my middle
and I am sharply aware
of my roundness,
the way my body
bulges now,
normally hidden
beneath my denim shirt
I try to shrink
shake you off
push away
with these damp hands
act too busy.
really, I am asking:

*how could you love
this part of me?*

// chosen

there is something
about those moments
when I allow myself
to melt
surrender to your
touch
fold into your arms
believe
at least for now
that your desire
is true.

// embracing you is embracing me

you see it all: these curves, rolls, lumps, dimples, bounces, wobbles -
some old, some new. I notice you watching me
and I freeze, wishing myself smaller, waiting for the punchline.
Instead, you pull me in, speaking with such healing tenderness
that I find myself slowly leaning into your gaze,
believing more and more that the beauty you see in me
is true, that hiding any part of this body
would never make me any more beautiful;
that the most loving and sacred dance
is between two souls who see each other fully,
know each other's stories,
can trace the other's scars with their eyes closed.

how lucky I am to be so seen and known.

// the healing of a lover's eyes

I see you, dear woman, as you stand
staring at the mirror, wondering when you began
to look so much like your mother -
tired and worn and more tender in some places,
tougher, in others

I watch your eyes as they
fall to your waistline and you remember a time
before so many years
stretched you -
it is hard in this moment to realize your true
magnificence, but I see it, wrapped
in that thick and glorious
story-skin you wear,
you are all beauty and scar and golden story
oh the memories this body holds -
if only you knew how
rich a tale your skin contains,
you might treat it with more kindness.

after all
you have been through so much life
together, but

it is easy to forget, because we have learned
from younger days to look at our bodies
with suspicion. we are strong and brilliant
princesses and mighty queens - until
someone points it out, and we notice
some sort of flaw,
we put our crown away
retreat to a tower
wait for someone to rescue
us, our worth hinging on their approval,
we begin to not trust our bodies

we hide them
shrink ourselves
reduce our belief in our worthiness
but you were
never meant
to be so small
and maybe
you just need someone
to remind you:

your body is good.

maybe today when you look in the mirror
you will turn away defeated,
but maybe tomorrow
you can look again
with a softness in your eyes and
thank your body
for carrying you so far –
along with everything
else the world has placed upon you –
and for creating your
story together.

// golden story

you may have heard
that mothers are allowed
to be selfish from time to time -
after all, we all need to be
seen
heard
loved
known
held.
don't you know
this isn't really
selfish at all?

// to be known

01. that I make time to nourish my body through food, movement, creativity.
02. that my children hear love in my voice, always.
03. that I stop apologizing for what I feel.
04. I make things both useful and beautiful with my own hands.
05. a heart brimming with gratitude.
06. a house filled with less things and more grace.
07. that we live somewhere new, for a little while.
08. that we nurture a sense of adventure and curiosity.
09. that I react less and embrace more.
10. and some new pillows would be nice, too.

// a mother's wish list (2 of 2)

if I could go back and mother myself
this is what I would do:

listen deeply to her dreams and desires
keep asking questions (even when it feels pointless)
teach her things for her own sake and enjoyment
know that when she screams, *I hate you*
she never really means it
and realize
she has already become
just as much
as she is still becoming.

// it's not too late to start

// them

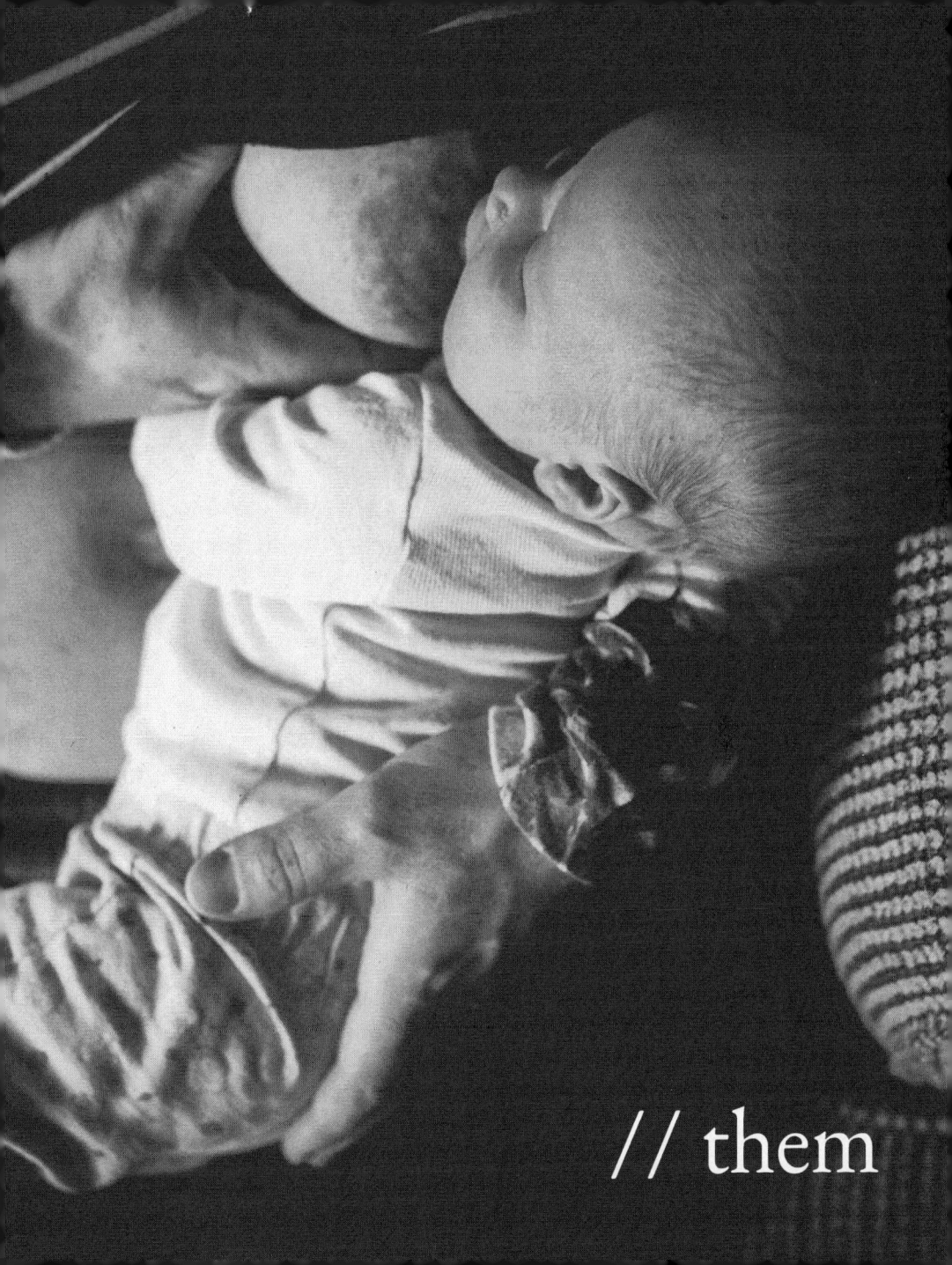

what they don't tell you
is the thing that
really keeps you
up at night
is whether you will be
enough

// no wonder mothers are always tired

here we are
you, soft in my arms
me, listing everything that
must be done
all the while
knowing someplace inside
that *this*
is the most important thing -
the thing that can't wait,
the thing that will be gone
before I can take another breath,
the thing I can never bring myself
to check off my list
for the final time.

// a mother's to-do list

motherhood is
memorizing
every little detail
while at the very
same moment
grieving it.

// enjoy the little things, they say

sometimes
I feel like I can see it -
I can see her
she stands strong
her face aligned
with the ground
looking straight ahead
at whatever is
there to meet her

she is
grounded
wise
ready
there is no knowing
what moments
of hard growth
or exquisite joy
she has faced
to get here -
there is so much
my hands have
no sway over

but

when I catch a glimpse
of this strong woman
I hope to meet
one day
it reminds me
of all the things
I wish I had known
when I was younger,
all the things

I wish someone had
been for me,
all the ways
I didn't see my
own worth and beauty.

I see you daughter
and I hope I can be
who you need
me to be.

// when my daughter is taller

where will you
go in life

what path will you choose

or

have chosen for you

how will we
have prepared you and

where will you
find all the
missing pieces
we leave
behind?

// reasonable questions

will I remember
what it was like
when your feet were this small?
when I held you
and you melted
into the crook of my arm
as we laid
on the aged cotton coverlet
spread across the bed
and I sang lulling melodies
to you, chin to cheek,
stroking your hair and peach-soft skin
as you nodded off to sleep.

you keep getting older
no matter how hard
I try to hold time back,
and my mother-heart is
crumpling in at the edges
as I tell myself
not to miss
my children so much
while they are still growing up.

// holding time or holding them

here you are
a babe
a boy
a man
still, in my arms
but grown as long
as these tired mama bones,
the ones that have been
carrying us both
all these years.
I don't even notice
the new person
greeting me in the
morning, the subtle
shift from child
to adult, from your
sweet small voice
whispering those
quiet secrets of
I love you
in my ear, to you now -
all gravel-toned and
moving further
and further away.

// leaving ho(me)

will you let me
grow among the flowers
and bloom
in the way I know how?

// all they really need from us

will I know how to love you
still, when you walk
in the same
grown-up places
I have been?

// growing together

there was something
about the way
she was laying there,
as the sun filtered
through the window
and warmed her,
golden curls
highlighted
in the bright rays,
a strawberry blonde
crescendo
softly falling
across her face.
I linger a moment
and watch -

watch her breathe

take in her small features
and rosy skin,
things I couldn't stop myself
from doing
when she hardly
had been outside
the womb a few days

but now
why is it so
much harder
to slow
and just look?

// before they fade away

it is a wretched gift
to be fully present
absorbing every detail
lingering
and
breathing
in deep
the sacred now
only to have
it become
a wispy memory
I can hardly
remember at all.

// why can't I stay in the moment forever

how easily we forget
to savor that look
in their eyes
that curve
in their lips
that smell
of their neck
that sensation
of their soft skin
against our own flesh.

// growing pains

you have your hands full
they casually comment
with an unwelcome wink and pause
waiting for some acknowledgment
I suppose,
have they commended me for my
strength and bravery, I wonder
or just had to point out how crazed I must look
out in public, just trying to buy some milk
and eggs without a meltdown in aisle 4.
I give a friendly chuckle and perhaps
too enthusiastic
of a reply
I sure do!, let the moment pass
continue to pick out
onions I'll cry over later.

we hear it so often, the women
the mothers
as if we didn't know
that we have been carrying more
than what feels fair
but we chose to have children
they say
and that is fine and true, or
perhaps we just chose to stay,
but our hands were full before
we ever took a child into our womb
or home,
many of us taught what our hands were good for
at an early age, already held
unattainable expectations for ourselves, already
navigating a world where shape shifting was required
where passion and anger are often confused
when coming from a woman's mouth.

what I wanted to say to the stranger
in the grocery store, over the kale
I would later hide in my children's spaghetti sauce:
you're right, my hands are so full
I am barely treading water
but I'm told wine and a nice soak
will make it better.
I haven't had a full night's sleep
in months, but coffee has been a close
friend to me and my anxiety
and somehow I'm supposed to raise
these humans who will fix this
world for themselves, but I don't even know
what's for dinner tonight
and there are hungry mouths
everywhere I turn.

other kind solicitors offer me more
words of wisdom:
this too will pass and *enjoy it while you can*
they say
because how unfortunate if you don't
bask in every moment of motherhood,
live for the night wakings and early mornings
right alongside the swells of joy
the ache of knowing you won't remember it all
once it's passed, and that you actually can't
hold it all anyway.

// a mother's hands

this is it.
this is it
THIS IS IT.

this moment,
his hand
irresistibly soft
wrapped around
my neck,
pulling my face
against that
not-quite-a-baby
but-still-soft-skin
cheek of his

how is it that I have to
convince myself to stay
and linger?
how can I not drop
everything to be here,
needed so preciously as
"mama"
in these quiet
moon-wrapped moments
before we bow to sleep?

// this could really be IT

those twinkling
watching
full-of-wonder eyes,
quietly absorbing
so much
when we are raw
and unedited,
not needing words
to understand
what we say to ourselves
while looking in mirrors
without moving lips,
as we suck in our waist
flip our hair
try to forget
what this tired skin
looks like -

we notice her
noticing us,
ask ourselves
does she understand her worth
how beautiful she is
and always will be -
the way I wish
I really believed
about myself?

// the silent messages we send

I want the world for you
while at the same moment
ache for you to be content
with simply being,
actually enjoy your
own company.
yet here I am
counting my flaws in the mirror
filling empty spaces
with tasks and scrolling,
busying myself so
I won't have to commune
with my own soul -

all while you look on.

// there is an entire world inside of you, too

I didn't mean it
when you came in
and I shouted,
when you just wanted
to know that I would
come to your side
be your safety net,
your help,
but I was tired and sore
and didn't listen long enough
to understand where
your heart was coming from.

you lean your head against my chest
now that we are quieter again,
my hands soften against your heartbeat
and I feel it.
I remember my own
small-girl-heart, remember
that we are just the same,
and there is a deep-sinking
sort of heaviness inside of me
knowing I made you feel
even for a moment
like you were somehow
less.

// trying to be their safe place

I always have grand
ideas of how
I will change myself
at 9pm at night -
but then the morning
nudges me awake
and the same old habits
join me at
the breakfast table.

// monday morning musings

small things matter.
peace begins in our homes,
starts with grace
for even ourselves
when we enter our day
already trying
to catch up.

// a redeeming presence

I never hear a mother
with grown children
remark
that she wished
she had spent less time
reading one more book
past bedtime,
painting tiny nails,
twirling in bedrooms
until you both fall, dizzy
and laughing
a fullness no words
describe

or how she wishes
she could take back
the hours spent
sitting on the floor
stacking blocks
and counting,
hiding behind doorways
waiting for tiny feet to find them
for the tenth or fifteenth time -
they are somehow just
as surprised and delighted
to discover their mama
as the first time
they pulled open
the door.

I never hear a mother
with grown children
regret
lingering after bedtime
to watch their child sleep,

their chest rising and falling
in a perfectly glorious cadence
or
picking up them up
as if it were
the last moment
their child
will be small enough
to carry in their arms.

we roll our eyes at them
these mothers, who speak with
story and memory thick in their eyes,
we meet them in the grocery store aisle
and library check-out
just trying to
make it back home -
maybe they are trying
to make it back
somewhere, too -
but we also feel
their sad-mother-wisdom
echo in our bones
and press against a tender
spot in our own
sad-mother-heart
knowing these young days,
while hard at times
won't last forever.

// before you know it

what do we get
when we listen to the advice
it will be over before you know it
when we pay such close attention
try to make sure we don't
miss a single thing?

I'm learning that
in the end,
we still find ourselves
missing those moments so
much it aches -
but I'd rather feel the happy ache
of those foggy, distant memories
than to have just been
sleepwalking through it all.

// the wonderful pain of loving you

I still remember
when you first said
love you, mama
and my heart soared
and ached
all at once.

// growing up

it was a sunny
July day
when you decided to
swap out the picture books
for ones with chapters
trade your pink sheets
for the old gray pinstriped ones
you found in the closet,
why, I ask inside
are you so eager
to grow up?
I bite my lip
and feel regret
for not holding you
a little longer
before bedtime,
singing more lullabies
and lingering as we
lay side-by-side, sharing
simple secrets in the dark

but I wonder
even if I could go back -
if I had known
how fast those long
days and nights would
actually go -
would I have done
anything different?

// a mother's haunting

// gift

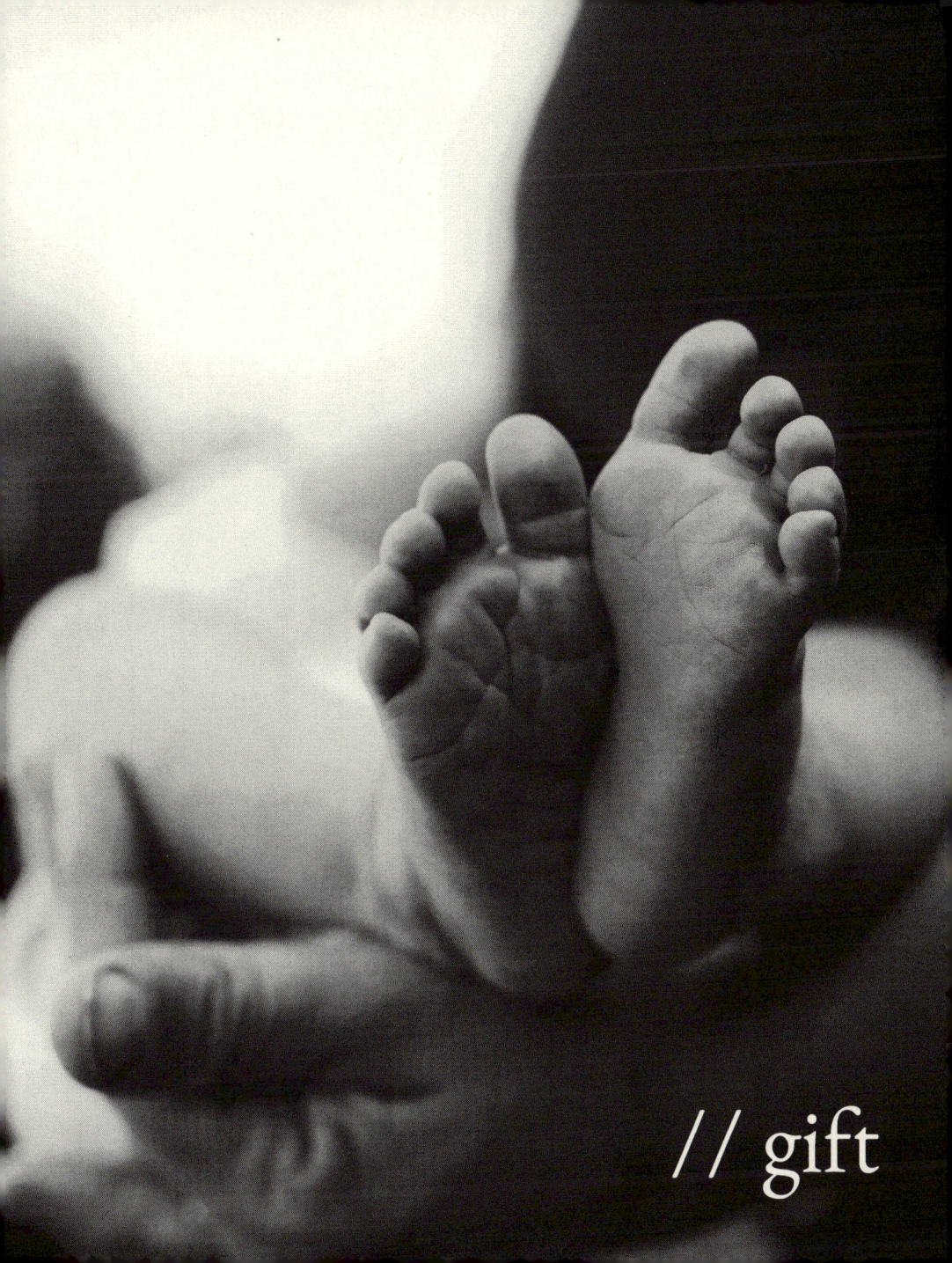

motherhood is
crowded & solitude
magic & impossible
hard & tender
home & much
too
short
a visit.

// don't blink

lately
I am noticing
how the task of
raising and
nourishing children
has so much more
to do
with my own transformation
than I ever thought.

// matrescence

how I wish mothers
everywhere
could see themselves
as they care
for their children
this magnificent
giving-of-self -
because there is so much
rich
hard
glorious
and
impossible
growth
that takes place
as we experience
this undoing,
this holy emptying
of ourselves
for the sake of another.

// we forget how much we give

as mothers, we are already
so familiar with the long, dark nights
aren't we. the ones that ask more
of us than we have to give, but
we somehow make it through, regardless -
eyes and limbs and hearts aching with
a tiredness only a mother knows,
the kind that makes us
wonder how we got here,
makes us feel unrecognizable
to even ourselves at times.

but the morning always comes,
eventually
and we see them -
these perfectly small
and fleshy babes of ours.
somehow, our bodies begin to forget
how long the night was
as that early-dawn-sun kisses us
with grace for a new day.

// in the light, everything shifts.

evening settles
I feel the
s h i f t
even without noticing
the dim hued light
s e e p
through
bedroom windows
we have blankets already
tucked tight
snug against chins
as we hold
each other close
nose
b r u s h e s
nose
fingers
l a c e
tight
heartbeats
s y n c
lips
s o f t e n
and the mistakes
from before
m e l t
in this perfect
moment of
f o r g i v e n e s s.

// nightly ritual of grace

we heal as
we turn toward others.

// turn softly

motherhood is
wrapping love
around yourself
and others
watching how
it changes you,
your world.

// invitation

mother, you are
star
moon
song
ancient carrier and protector
warm center and home
provider and nurturer
tender soul
and fierce holder of life,
you shine with grace
and a rawness also
that is far too beautiful,
some cannot bear it
they turn away
tell you to tone it down -
but how can you keep hidden
the very essence of
who you are?

show your scars along
with your glory
share your brilliance
the moon and sun
within you,
there is no way to
name all that you do
or sing your song
to completion,
it would stretch across ages
into the next life.

you hold a joy
that only surrender
and letting go
and great grief allow,

for a mother's love
is a hard and ferocious thing,
this un-doing
and re-making of self.

// a mother's psalm

oh mother
do you see yourself?
do you know what you give
and sustain?
do you see that even when
you feel like a failure
or let yourself down
your sacrifices matter?
these early days can seem
so long and short
and it is a creeping
suddenness
that comes when you
look down one day
at your sleeping babe,
notice how long
she has grown already -
you recall the smallness
and bigness
of those newborn days
and wonder where they went.
there are so many
unseen moments
which no one may ever
thank you for,
but how I desire for you to see
the love
in your hands
as you care for and clothe
your child,
feed and nourish
bounce and
rock and
sway and
sing to them, let them know

from the very beginning
how worthy of love they are.

// you are amazing

maybe
we just need to
remember
to enter the smallness
of our day
in big ways -
to zip up coats
wipe noses
brush hair
with a fierce
core of love.

// small things matter

thank you
for showing me
what life is,
how to slow down
and see
with eyes and
heart wide
open,
to feel with every
bit of me -
even letting the sad parts
drip and leak
when they need to,
and still know
I am whole.

// you teach me so much

how do we walk
with tender hands
in a world that seems
so stiff and lost?
maybe it starts here
in this rough-and-gentle
melting-of-self we encounter
when we learn
to love another
as if they were our own,
when we cry for their pain
rally for their freedom
cheer them on
like a fierce and
unstoppable mother
who believes deeply
in their child's worth,
who will give everything
they have away
if it means
their loved one
could simply rest
and breathe easy
in this world
for even one day.

// we are all their mothers

perhaps this is why
we are left so strong
and soft, broken and open:

once you have loved someone
that you see so much of
yourself in, there is opportunity
to learn to love
in the very
hardest
way.

// love others as [you learn to love] yourself

ACKNOWLEDGMENTS

Thank you most to my long-time partner, husband, co-parent and cheerleader, Jer Ellis, who has believed in me and my voice since we first met. Thank you for the hours to work in solitude, knowing exactly how to set up the perfect atmosphere when I need a bath, and the reminders of my inherent worth and loveliness. To my children who have taught me how to love - you are forever my greatest teachers. There are so many who are dear to me who have encouraged and supported me to keep writing and sharing my words, both in small and big ways. A few of those names include: Nikki Parnell, Joslyn Walker, Morgan Schmidt, Shea Kluender, Lexy Deitchler, Amanda McDermott; my dear sister-in-loves, Tawny Ellis and Hanna Salas; my brother, Kit Merker. And the many readers who have been following along on my Instagram account since 2019 - you helped me see there was space in the world for my words, too. There aren't sufficient words, but thank you - I am forever grateful.

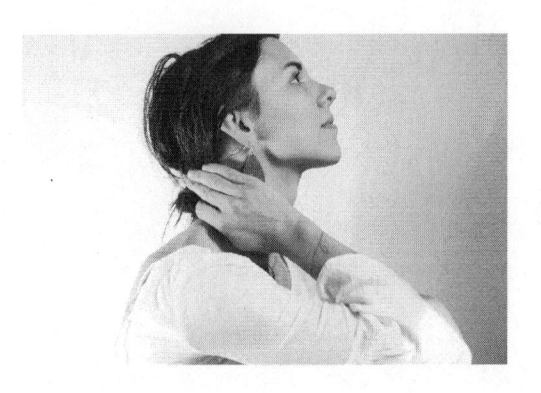

AUTHOR BIO

bec ellis is a poet, writer, photographer and helpless creative who is invested in following the threads of connection through vulnerability in both her writing and conversation with others. She often writes on themes of embodiment, self-compassion, and motherhood, longing for words that help bring healing to herself and others. She lives with her partner and their three children in Central Oregon.

instagram: @bec_ellis_writer
web: www.bec-ellis.com